A Brief Overview of Annuities

By Kirk G. Meyer

A Brief Overview of Annuities

Copyright © 2014 by Kirk G. Meyer

Why I Wrote this Book

I am a licensed life insurance agent who can sell
fixed annuities through various life insurance
companies I represent, though currently, I am a
fiduciary fee-only financial advisor not selling any
products. I wanted to understand these complex
financial products better. So what better way to
understand annuities than do the research that was
needed to write this book. There is a whole world
that revolves around annuities, and it is much more
complex and complicated than will be discussed in
this short book. But in writing this book, I did gain
a better understanding of annuities, how they work,
who they are designed for, and who can best benefit
from purchasing one.

Why You Should Buy this Book

Anyone who is thinking about buying any annuity needs to understand what it is that they are buying fully. While this book does not go into every type of annuity available or all of the riders that can be associated with an annuity, it does provide some of the essential basics. No one should ever buy a financial product that they do not understand. As I found out as an annuity salesman and while researching this book, only people who deal with these products regularly can even really begin to understand them. That is not to say that you cannot prepare yourself to the best of your ability. You can, and this book should be your first step in that direction. A Brief Overview of Annuities can assist anyone who is considering purchasing any type of annuity product.

My Gift to You

As a big thank you for getting A Brief Overview of Annuities, I want to offer you some valuable gifts and a chance to get some on-going financial advice.

Just for getting this book, it entitles you to my
Budget Spreadsheet and Debt Reduction
Spreadsheet that I normally sell for a total of $10. It
is yours free for getting A Brief Overview of
Annuities and signing up for my free email
newsletters that have previews to my ebooks. These
special articles are geared towards personal finance
and now access to these two useful spreadsheets. To
get your spreadsheets, now go to my blog's website
and sign up today. Visit http://bit.ly/KGMLetter
today to get your free valuable spreadsheets.

Table of Contents

Introduction

Before we delve into the history, some of the types of annuities, and what makes them unique, let's first examine some of the basics about why people in today's society purchase an annuity. First and foremost, an annuity will provide you, your spouse, or someone else a periodic payment for the rest of your life or a specific period. Some annuities provide a certain degree of death benefits to your named beneficiary as well. And one of the most widely used reasons is that your money will grow tax-deferred until you withdraw the funds, at which time you will pay ordinary income taxes on the difference between what you invested and the growth of the value of the annuity. In the United States, there are three different types of annuities sold. However, there are several variations of each type, depending on what guarantees or riders you purchase in conjunction with your annuity. The three main types are fixed annuity, variable annuity, or indexed annuity.

History of Annuities

Annuities have existed in one form or another dating back to the Roman Empire but have only looked as they now do for the last several decades. Since they date back to the age of the Roman Empire, the word annuity, derived from the Latin word annua, which means annual stipends, and during this time, mainly soldiers would make a large payment in exchange for annual payments for the rest of their lives or a specific number of years. Also, at this time, a Roman citizen Gnaeus Domitius Annius Ulpianis, is cited as one of the earliest dealers in annuities and is also credited with developing the first actuarial life tables. (Milevsky, 2013)

Skipping ahead to the Middle Ages, annuities were used by feudal lords and royalty to help offset the costs of constant wars and conflicts with one another. During this period, annuities were offered as tontines, which was a large pool of cash from which made payments to a pool of people who invested in the tontine. As people died off, the resulting payments to the surviving investors increased until one person was the sole survivor and thus received the entire pool of money. (Rettick, 2011) In Europe, annuities continued to be used to fund wars, provide for royal families, and other purposes. In later centuries annuities were popular investments for wealthy individuals who were looking for the safety of annuities as investments. From the beginning until the 18th Century, all of the annuities cost the same regardless of individual factors. At this point, age and gender became factors in the issuance and cost of an annuity. What the issuers of annuities saw was that the recipients of annuities lived longer than those who did not receive them, and they then began adjusting the price of annuities based on age and gender.

The first annuities in America were introduced around 1760 when in Pennsylvania, they used annuities for church pastors. These first American annuities were funded mainly by the pastor and his church congregation to provide a safe and secure income for the pastors and their families for life. Over time annuities have caught on in American society, and Benjamin Franklin left an annuity to the cities of Boston and Philadelphia. The Boston annuity lasted until the 1990's when the city opted for a lump sum payment of the annuity. (Milevsky, 2013) In more recent memory, annuities have begun to catch on with the general public. This slow adoption of the annuity came about because, in days past, people in America felt as if they could rely on their extended family for support. So during this period, annuities were mainly used by attorneys and executors of estates as a means of providing for beneficiaries of last wills and testaments. In America, annuities did not become commercially available until 1812, when a Pennsylvania life insurance company started marketing them available to the general public. President Lincoln was a supporter of using annuities as a form of payment to soldiers, as opposed to land grants, to provide injured and wounded soldiers a payment source.

In America, the multigenerational households have declined, which has led to annuities seeing an increase in the early 20th Century. After the stock market crash of 1929, numerous individuals were directed towards annuities as they were looking for safer investment opportunities. With the increased interest in annuities, life insurance companies looking for ways to "improve" annuities, and in 1952 unveiled the first variable annuity. (Watkins) Since that time, life insurance companies have incorporated various riders, benefits, and features in both fixed and variable annuities. A popular annuity was introduced in the late 1980s, called the indexed annuity; these products have also evolved ever since their inception and since being offered to the general public. (Rettick, 2011) Between the mid-1860s and 1920, annuities accounted for 1.5% of all life insurance premiums collected, and in 2011 it was estimated that annuity sales exceeded

$200 billion on an annual basis. Although annuities first started as simple investment type instruments, they have become very complex products, which are some of the most misunderstood, misused, and abused financial instruments in today's markets.

Modern Annuities

As a financial tool, an annuity has different phases or aspects of its life cycle. Modern annuities have three distinct phases, those being the accumulation, annuitization, and payout phases. It is noted that not all annuities will have all three of these phases, depending on what product is purchased, when it is purchased, and the purpose of the annuity purchased. For example, an annuity that is funded with a lump-sum payment and set to begin immediate payments would not necessarily have an accumulation phase.

The accumulation phase is always the first phase of an annuity and is the period of growth for the annuity after the initial payment is received. The accumulation phase will last until the payments begin on the annuity. In some instances, annuities are funded in lump sums, and in others, are funded over some time. Still, until the payments begin, the annuity is in the accumulation phase. Annuitization is when the annuity is converted from the accumulation phase into the payment phase and is a point in time more than an actual phase or period. This point is when the insurance company will begin to make payments to the individual who purchased the annuity. If the annuity purchased was a variable annuity, this is the point in time when the units purchased converted into annuity units for payment purposes. The third and final phase is the payout phase, and that is when the money accumulated over some time is paid out to the purchaser of the annuity. The payout phase may be brief or very long, depending on the type of product that was purchased, how well funded it is, the rate of return, and the desired longevity required by the individual who purchased the annuity in the first place.

It should be noted that during the payout phase, an annuity will continue to accumulate interest or gains while making the payouts. This is done in all annuities, regardless of type, and will occur in fixed, indexed, and variable annuities all the same. An annuity will continue to accumulate some rate of return until making the last payout payment, the annuity is exhausted, and no more money remains in the vehicle. There are several options for funding annuities, with the most popular being a single payment, fixed premium, and flexible premium. A single payment is a lump sum payment used to fund the annuity at a single point in time. Fixed premiums are a series of payments to the life insurance company over a fixed period and for a fixed amount used to fund the annuity until fully funded. A flexible premium is one that normally has a minimum amount that needs to be funded but also allows for the payment of extra funds when the investor can, or can afford, additional payments to fund the annuity.

While there are mainly three ways to fund an annuity, there are several ways in which payments are made. One is the straight life method in which an individual will receive a set payment for as long as he lives, regardless of whether the value of the annuity is exhausted or not. This is a good deal for the individual if he lives for a longer period in the payout phase as compared to the funded amount of the annuity; however, if the individual dies before receiving his entire investment, the remaining money is normally returned to the life insurance company, thereby giving both parties some risk in this type of transaction. Life income with refund is where the individual who has purchased the annuity will receive income for her life. If she dies before receiving the entire purchase amount, leaving any remaining funds to a beneficiary. There is a cost to this benefit, and it is a lower payout than straight life because now the insurance company knows it will owe any remaining money to the beneficiary. It will not go back to the life insurance company.

Another group of annuity payouts starts with life income with a certain period, where a person is guaranteed a fixed payment for a set number of years. In the event he dies before the contract expires, he can leave the remaining payments to a beneficiary. Again this feature comes with a cost, and it will lower the payments that will be received. A joint-life annuity is just like a straight life annuity, but in this instance, there are two annuitants to receive payments. In this payout, payments will continue as long as both annuitants are alive and will cease when one dies, making this a seldom-used payment method. Joint survivor life is a much more popular choice, as it will pay a set amount as long as both annuitants are alive and will then normally pay a reduced amount on the death of one of the annuitants. Again this feature comes at a cost and will have a lower payout than straight life.

Period certain begins another group of payment options, and it will pay for a set number of years until the contract is exhausted and no more funding remains. This is a very simple annuity in design and appears to be popular with individuals. Joint survivor life with period certain is a combination of joint life and joint survivor life options. This payout will continue until both annuitants are dead, at which time the beneficiary will receive any remaining funds in the annuity until the set period is exhausted. A fixed amount of payment is when an annuitant will receive a set payment until the funds are exhausted, regardless of time. This is also a very simple annuity and set up to have a beneficiary receive any funds that may be left after the annuitant dies.

Individuals who buy annuities seldom buy a simple straight life annuity without some sort of option or rider associated with it. The more options or riders added to an annuity in the form of options, the more the annuity will cost, and those increased fees will lower any future payouts. But many insurance companies now offer very flexible payouts that may even change after annuitization to allow annuity owners greater flexibility in the payments they will receive.

The next process in an annuity is the timing of the annuitant's payout. As a general rule, they are divided into one of two types, immediate or deferred. In an immediate payout, the annuity does not have an accumulation phase before any payments beginning. As the name implies, the payments will begin as soon as the annuity is funded, generally with a lump sum payment. A deferred annuity principal is invested over some time between an initial payment or lump sum payment until the annuity will begin a payment schedule.

An annuity involves four interested parties, and in some instances, a person may fill more than one role. First is the contract owner; this is the individual who buys the annuity and pays the premiums. As a general rule, the contract owner is normally the same individual as the annuitant. The annuitant is the person who will receive the payments of the annuity. If the annuity has survivorship rights or is a fixed-term annuity, there will be a beneficiary for the annuity. And finally, there is the life insurance company that issues the annuity and is responsible for its payments.

Frequently, individuals may consider an annuity in their retirement planning; some of the advantages that make an annuity attractive and unique are as follows. One of the main advantages of an annuity is its tax-deferred status. While other investments may have tax deferral status, annuities do not have limitations on how much can be placed in them to grow, and also, there are no limitations on the income they can produce. You cannot say the same of Individual Retirement Accounts (IRAs) or 401(k) accounts that do grow tax-deferred but are limited to as to the amount contributed in any tax year. This makes annuities attractive for people who are looking to shelter large sums of money for tax purposes to help in their retirement. Annuities provide a guaranteed payout and, in some instances, may pay out more than the annuitant has paid in contributions and/or in accumulated value. The next two advantages may not be the same from state to state, but as a rule, annuities are exempt from creditors and probate estate upon the annuitant's death. Also, parents and students are not required to list annuities on their Free Application for Federal Student Aid (FAFSA) forms, which can help a student in obtaining federal assistance for qualified college expenses. And finally, if set up correctly, an annuity can be owned and excluded from your assets when Medicaid steps in to assist with nursing home expenses.

Unlike the advantages, which are fairly uniform from individual to individual, disadvantages also exist. The major disadvantages of annuities are as follows. The first major disadvantage to annuities is the numerous costs and fees associated with ownership. As a rule, annuities are one of the most expensive investments available to individuals, and these fees will be looked at later. Also, annuities are not considered to be liquid, and almost all of them carry steep surrender charge penalties and a

10% early distribution fee for withdrawing money before the age of 59½. One exception is that some allow a withdrawal of up to 10% of the annuity without penalty, depending on the annuity and the life insurance company who issued it. While some annuities are very simple in design, many can be very complex and very difficult to understand, especially indexed and variable types. Annuities are also taxed differently than regular retirement accounts where your principal is returned to you tax-free since, in theory, you have already paid taxes on that money. Still, any interest or gains will be taxed as ordinary income and not as a less expensive long-term capital gain.

As mentioned earlier, annuities have surrender charges associated with them, and these can be as high as 15% and last as long as ten years. (Weisman, 2009) In practice, the charge will decrease over the stated period until there is no charge left for an early surrender. In most instances, there are certain conditions when the surrender fees are waived, and they are as follows. If the annuitant experiences a medical emergency, hardship, or disability, most companies will waive the surrender fee and allow the annuitant to some or all of their money early. As noted earlier as well, many companies will allow a partial withdrawal, normally up to 10% a year, until the surrender charge is exhausted. And all annuities will offer a certain number of days for new annuitants to review the policy and make sure it is indeed what they want and need; this is called a Free Look Period. This period may vary from state to state, and in the event of a variable annuity, the Securities and Exchange Commission (SEC) has said they shall provide ten or more days for this.

Since an annuity is a retirement type investment, it is subject to the 10% penalty, the same as an IRA or 401(k) if withdrawn before age 59½. This is a penalty that will be assessed to any early withdrawal by an annuitant, and the life insurance company or issuing company may also impose its penalty. Annuitants must also start taking payouts when they reach age 70½, the same as a traditional IRA or 401(k) if you are no longer working. If you reach age 70½ and do not take a payout, there will be a 50% penalty imposed on the amount that you were due to take out. These are implications that are placed on annuities by the Internal Revenue Service (IRS) and not by the life insurance companies.

While in America, only a life insurance company can issue an annuity; numerous groups market them. Some groups that market annuities are banks, life insurance agents and brokers, stockbrokers and Registered Investment Advisors, financial planners, estate and trust officers, and mutual fund companies. Regardless of who is marketing an annuity, the person who sells it must be a licensed life insurance agent from the state in which they are selling the annuity. In the case of variable annuities, the person selling needs to be a licensed life insurance agent as well as a registered securities dealer.

While annuities do have their place in an individual's retirement planning, they are not for everyone. These are extremely complex and complicated instruments and are commonly misunderstood and, in many instances, miss-marketed to potential buyers. Two reasons for this are that first, many sell annuities as a "one size fits all" for someone's retirement when that may not be the case, and the second is that annuities have some of the highest commissions of any investment product available. The payout to the person who sells an annuity can be anywhere from 4% to 15%, leading many who sell these to be biased when selling to customers and potential customers. (Milevsky, 2013) Indexed annuities have received a majority of the negative publicity because of high surrender fees and the targeting of seniors by those who sell them. In many instances, the sellers of these annuities encourage seniors to place liquid assets into an IRA or qualified plan when there is no need to do this, as the annuity is already tax-deferred and mainly considered illiquid.

With regard to regulation, most annuities are regulated at the state level since a life insurance license is required to sell them in any state. In the case of fixed and indexed annuities, the state is the sole regulator, as these instruments are not considered as securities and therefore fall outside the jurisdiction of the SEC. All states have an Insurance Commission that oversees the life insurance and annuity activities within that state— in addition to state regulation. They are also defined and governed by the Internal Revenue Code. The SEC and Financial Industry Regulatory Authority (FINRA) oversee the sale of variable annuities, as they are considered securities and require a securities license, in addition to a life insurance license, to sell. Currently, indexed annuities are not considered securities, but this may change as their status is evaluated since they do participate in the equities market gains.

Prior to a discussion of the different types of annuities, there are some basic questions one needs to answer before choosing and buying an annuity. Anyone who is considering an annuity needs to have individual retirement goals and financial needs in mind when looking at any of the three types of annuities. Some of the questions to ask include the following.

• What are the goals for the money I will place in the annuity?

• How much risk can I tolerate with the money I am putting in the annuity?

• Do I have enough funds outside of the annuity for emergencies and living expenses?

• How long will I be able to leave the money in the annuity to ensure I avoid early termination fees and surrender fee charges?

This is not a comprehensive list of the questions that are important to ask before buying an annuity, but they are some of the most common ones. Perhaps the main question regards risk tolerance, which will help determine which of the three types of annuities is the right choice for you.

Types of Annuities

There are three basic types of annuities—fixed, indexed, and variable. A fixed annuity is appropriate for a more conservative investor who is looking to have a guarantee on the principal and interest earned. Indexed annuities are more appropriate for moderate investors who, in theory, want the benefits of the markets without the risk of losing the principal. Variable annuities are appropriate for moderate to more aggressive investors who are willing to risk the principal in a retirement account; these annuities also have the possibility for much higher returns than the previous two types of annuities. For conservative investors who still want a variable annuity, they can, for an additional fee, purchase a rider that will guarantee the income. While there are three basic types, any one of the three can have one or more riders added to meet the specific needs of the annuitant.

A fixed annuity has a guarantee to return the principal as well as a stated fixed rate of return and acts much like a certificate of deposit though it grows tax-deferred. One of the chief advantages of a fixed annuity is the interest rate it pays. A fixed annuity generally pays a higher interest rate than a certificate of deposit, treasury, or savings bond. Many fixed annuities will offer teaser rates to individuals to sell them, and then drop the guaranteed rate after a set period, for the remainder of the annuity. Individuals who shop around for better deals in fixed annuities also need to be aware of the financial condition of the life insurance company selling the annuity. Essential, as many annuities are spread over decades, and as an investor, you are not only buying a fixed rate of return on your annuity, you are purchasing a long-term asset from a company, and you need some assurance that the life insurance company is in good financial standing. While most states require life insurance companies to belong to the state's guaranty association to step in and pay a portion of an annuity in the event the life insurance company fails, you should not count on this as protection of your entire annuity. Individuals need to make sure the company is financially sound before purchasing any annuity.

The difference between a fixed annuity and an indexed annuity is that in an indexed annuity, you will benefit from the movements in an index tied to an equity market or markets. An indexed annuity has the characteristics of both a fixed annuity and a variable annuity, discussed later. Like a fixed annuity, it offers a guarantee on your principal, but the rate of return is not set. It can fluctuate from year to year or period to period, based on the index that the annuity tracks (mainly the S&P 500). An annuity with an annual reset is credited with the rate of return each year that the market exceeds its previous year's closing level. In the event, there is no positive gain in the index, the individual's annuity is not credited with any gains. Still, then again, it is not debited any of the losses, the principal in an indexed annuity is guaranteed. A point to point will measure the index from the start of the period to the end, which is normally five years. An annual reset annuity can calculate index gains on the average for the year and not the simple difference between the beginning of the period and the end of it, thereby possibly creating a lower return for the buyer. Therefore, an indexed annuity is slightly riskier than a fixed annuity but has much less risk than a variable annuity. Also, many fixed and indexed annuities will charge a fee or a spread subtracted from the annuity's return before being applied to the annuity's balance.

Most indexed annuities will contain at least one of the following features, and many will contain several. One of these features is a minimum guaranteed return that the annuity will pay

31

regardless of whether the index produces a positive return. Generally, this fixed guaranteed return rate will be much lower than the fixed annuity, but still better than a negative return or no return at all. The guaranteed minimum may typically be 87.5% of the premium paid at a 1% to 3% interest rate. Another feature of an indexed annuity is a cap rate, which means there is a maximum return that the annuity will pay in the event there are large movements in the index itself. Another way around this is that the indexed annuity will pay a percentage of the index's gain for the year and not 100% of the gain. As an example, your annuity's cap rate is 7%, and the index returned a 10% return, applying only 7% to the annuity. In other words, if the index goes above the cap rate or there is a percentage paid on the index's gain, the remaining funds go to the life insurance company and not the purchaser of the annuity.

Please note, not all annuities have a cap rate, but most do, so when buying an annuity, always read and understand what is being purchased. Also, some indexed annuities have a floor, which is the minimum the insurance company will pay, usually 0%. But all indexed annuities will have a minimum guaranteed value or interest rate. For the insurance company to be able to offer indexed annuities, they will invest a portion of the principal in derivatives that pay generously when the market moves in the correct direction, as the principal of the derivative and a portion in a guaranteed investment. This way, a portion will normally exceed the index, and in the event the index is negative, the guaranteed portion will provide for the minimum rate of return.

Also in an indexed annuity, the percentage paid to the annuitant is called the participation rate. Depending on the issuing life insurance company, it will determine the participation rate of your principal. This rate can be set for the entire length of the annuity, or it may have another term, such as an annual change. The way this works, say the index gained 10% for that period, or the cap rate if less than the total return, and the participation rate is

75%, making your actual gain 7.5%, or 10% times 75%. Insurance companies can set the participation rate daily, so when the annuity is purchased, it will determine what the participation rate will be for the annuity as well if it has a reset feature.

When it comes to determining the index's average, there are several different ways in which the insurance company can calculate the amount paid. Some annuities will use the averaging method, e.g., average the index return over some time instead of using fixed dates. Others will use the start and end dates of a set period and will calculate any possible gains in the change from the beginning to the end of the period. Each type has its advantages and disadvantages, so be sure to understand the calculation of the percentage gain and be comfortable with whatever means used. Averaging allows the annuity to spread all gains and losses over a set period, making good days and bad days offset each other, and the number of each will determine a gain or loss. While the period to period method will have a starting level and an ending level, the gain is the spread between the two if it is positive. This method allows the annuitant to take advantage of large declines in the index. As an example, if the index starts at 1100 and ends at 850, you will receive your guaranteed rate of return, but say the next period the index goes from 850 to 1300, your possible gain is larger due to the dramatic increase in the index. Your return will also depend on the cap if there is one.

Another feature of indexed annuities is averaging, which is where the value of the index is averaged, instead of the actual annuity's value on a specific date. The averaging of the annuity can occur at the beginning, end, or throughout the life of the annuity. The interest earned on the annuity can be simple or compounded interest. Simple interest means the value of the interest is calculated once during the term on a specific date and applied to the value of the annuity. If compounding the interest, the interest earned during the period will be added to the value of the annuity. It will then create a new annuity base in which interest is paid during the term. In both cases, the interest earned during the period will be applied to the old base to create a new base, which will then earn interest during the next term. Some annuities have a vesting period where the interest earned will not all be available in the event a withdrawal is made from the annuity. Once the vesting period is over, 100% of the gains will be available to the owner of the annuity. So check the annuity purchased to determine if there is a vesting period, and if so, how long the vesting period is, and consider that.

There are three main ways in which an indexed annuity will vary. Some have an annual reset, determining the interest rate earned by taking the starting point of the index and the ending point on an annual basis, and the positive difference would determine the return. Your gains are locked in each year in this method. The second method is the high-water mark, where the highest point of the index by comparing the term to the start and that difference, if positive, is your gain in the index. This method helps to protect your annuity against declines, but if you withdraw funds before the anniversary date, you may lose those gains. And finally, the point to point method is simply the difference between the two points of the term, and if the value is positive, that is the percentage your annuity will be credited. An advantage of this method is normally a higher cap and participation rate. In all three cases, caps may apply, and if the return is negative, crediting you with your minimum guaranteed rate of return for your annuity. Also, in an indexed annuity, dividends are not passed on to the owners of the annuity, so you will not be able to participate in the gains that dividends provide.

While many insurance salesmen will state that you cannot lose money in an indexed annuity, it is possible provided certain things occur. Remember that if the guaranteed rate is only applied to 87.5% of the premium and the interest rate is 1% to 3%, in theory, a loss on the investment could occur if the indexed rate does not come into play. Another way to lose money in an indexed annuity is by having to pay surrender charges if the money is needed early.

Variable annuities are perhaps the most complex and, not surprisingly, the most expensive of the three types of annuities to purchase. Of all of the financial instruments available to the individual retail investor, they are among the most complex. Before buying a variable annuity, be prepared to ask your insurance agent or broker many questions about the annuity being sold. Basically, in a variable annuity, the investor picks and chooses what mutual fund accounts to invest in, intending to get the largest possible gains for the individual annuity. Additionally, it normally has a life insurance component or death benefit that further adds to its expensive fees. (Watkins) All of the gains from the selected funds grow tax-deferred, as is the case with all annuities.

What makes variable annuities so complex is the relationship between the funds an investor can select from and the life insurance company's selection of mutual funds for the annuity. That, combined with all of the various riders and other benefits that are common with variable annuities, makes them truly complex. Many of the riders are designed to reduce the risk associated with the variable annuity. Still, by reducing the risk with these riders, the associated fees increase with the annuity's ownership. One such rider that is expensive to attach to the annuity is one that can guarantee the investor's principal as well as set the rate of return. And the investor is not the only part of the annuity that is protected, as many beneficiaries will receive a death benefit of the current contract value, the highest anniversary value, or a hypothetical amount based on a fixed interest rate if the current value is less than the calculated amount.

Many of a variable annuity's fees are charged to the annuity on a quarterly or annual basis. Most of the following fees are associated with a variable annuity.

• Mortality and expense charges are standard fees that are found in all variable annuities and cover the death provisions commonly found in most variable annuities.

• Contingent deferred sales charges are back-end charges which decline to zero over the life of the annuity, usually by 1% over 10 years, resulting in a 10% back-end loaded fund.

• Administrative service charges cover the money management fees associated with the different mutual funds and the management of your funds, should you opt for the life insurance company to do things such as rebalance your account.

• Contract maintenance charges are fees that cover the general maintenance of the annuity.

• Fund expenses cover the fees charged by mutual funds within the annuity, including the 12b-

1 fees and other management-related fees associated with the running of the individual mutual funds. On average, an annuity with many of these features can expect fees between 2-3% per year and, in many instances, much higher. (Watkins) The more riders an annuity has, the more in fees are charged to the owner of the annuity. There is also an administrative fee of around $25 per year, or it could be 0.15% of the annuity, depending on the insurance company's policy on administrative fees. Now, more and more life insurance companies are offering to unbundle these riders and are allowing the investor to pick and choose which riders they prefer in their annuities. Remember that variable annuities are meant to be long-term investments, so these fees will be paid for the life of the annuity, resulting in their high expense costs.

Unlike the fixed and indexed annuity, a variable annuity allows the investor to pick and choose how to invest the annuity premiums. The insurance company invests the money paid in mutual funds.

Either you or an agent at the insurance company will decide and invest in certain sectors and funds offered by the insurance company. While these mutual funds are similar to those offered to the average retail investor, there are indeed subtle differences, since, by law, the funds must be separate for retail investors and investors through an annuity. The key to a successful variable annuity is to understand the funds you are investing in, and that means reading and understanding the prospectus of each fund selected.

A common feature of a variable annuity is that there typically is a life insurance component to the death benefit. The mortality expense charged to the annuitant is normally in the range of 1.25% on an annual basis. In the event of the annuitant's death, the beneficiary would receive the greater of the money left in the annuity or the guaranteed minimum, such as all of the payments you made during the accumulation phase minus any payouts received. A rider that is related to the death benefit is one that will guarantee minimum income benefits or a minimum level of annuity payments, even if you do not have enough money in the annuity to cover the payments. Another feature that is available to variable annuities is long-term care riders, which will pay for nursing home expenses if the annuitant becomes seriously or terminally ill. When looking at a variable annuity with these types of riders, it is extremely important to do plenty of research and ensure the life insurance company is financially sound and will be able to pay these riders, as in many instances, they are paying out benefits above the premiums paid by the annuitant and over an extended period.

Conclusion

In the event you want to change insurance companies and do not wish to pay the taxes associated with any gains, Section 1035 of the U.S. tax code allows for this to occur. This provision allows for a tax-deferred annuity used to purchase another without incurring the taxes on the gains of the first annuity. Section 1035 can be beneficial if you have an annuity that is past the surrender period, and you find another that may have better benefits, and you would like to change companies. If you are still within the surrender period, you will have to do the math and figure out if the change is worth the cost.

Also, many insurance companies will offer a bonus for you to buy their annuity. These bonuses can typically be between 1% and 5% of the purchase cost. But, as in life, nothing is free, and so it is with this type of bonus. One way they can recoup the cost is higher and longer surrender charges in the event you need to withdraw your money. These annuities often will charge higher mortality and expense to annuitants who received a bonus to open their accounts. And finally, on bonuses, they are normally only applied to the initial amount you invested in the first year of the accumulation phase. So make sure the bonus outweighs the extra fees and longer periods you receive, or you may be better off declining the bonus from the start.

Regardless of the type of annuity you decide to purchase. It would be best if you asked several questions of the insurance agent or the issuing company.

• What is the guaranteed minimum interest rate for the annuity?

• Are there any charges deducted from my premium for the annuity?

• Are there any charges deducted from my contract value in the annuity?

• How long is the term of the annuity?

- If there is a participation rate for the annuity, what is it? Is the participation rate guaranteed? Is there a minimum participation rate for the annuity?
- Is there a cap on what the annuity could earn, and if so, what is it?
- Does the annuity use averaging, and how does that work in detail?
- How is interest on the annuity calculated? Is the interest simple or compounded, and how often is it computed?
- Are there any administrative fees, a spread, or margin in addition to, or instead of, the participation rate?
- Which indexing method is used in the annuity?
- What are the surrender charges if I need to withdraw my money early, and how do they work?
- Is there a vesting period for my annuity?
- Can I make a partial withdrawal without any penalty of losing interest or additional principal?
- Is there a nursing home or critical illness exception to withdrawals?

- What payment options are available for the annuity?

- Is there a death benefit for the annuity?

While annuities can be relatively simple or very complex, they may have a place in your retirement planning. Depending on your level of sophistication, you can go with a generic fixed annuity if you are conservative, an indexed annuity (if more risk is not an issue) that could return more than a fixed annuity but with more fees and riders available, or a variable annuity which does offer the most risk and highest returns but also are among the most complex financial instruments available, as well as being some of the most expensive. As with any financial instrument, anyone who purchases an annuity needs to do their research, not only on the annuity and any riders it contains but the life insurance company that issues the annuity, since the annuity may be around for decades to fulfill the obligations. If used properly, an annuity can be a good supplement for guaranteed income in your retirement years, or you may accumulate large sums of money and have it grow tax-deferred until retirement, and then benefit from a steady stream of income during this time. But due to their complexity and the nature of the fees associated with them, they are not for everyone though many annuity salespeople sell them to individuals who may not understand them or be able to afford the annuity, its restrictions, or high fees.

One area that deserves consideration in your retirement plans is how an annuity can aid in the planning for nursing home care and the assistance of Medicaid. There is a very specific type of annuity used in Medicaid planning, and that is an immediate irrevocable annuity and is not a tax-deferred annuity. (Takacs) These annuities must be actuarially sound before they are valid under the Medicaid rules set by individual states. Before entering into a Medicaid-friendly annuity, consider the following needs before its purchase. First, it is an irrevocable annuity, so make sure you will need the annuity for the stated period. Second, it should only be purchased to protect the assets of the spouse's share of the couple's assets. Buying an annuity is not the only way to achieve this, so look at all options before purchasing an annuity, and consult with a financial planner or estate planner. Also, while federal laws and rules allow for such annuities, states have attacked them in recent years; check the rules in your state regarding Medicaid-friendly annuities before you buy one, and be aware that your state could change the way it views them after you have made your purchase.

So there are several valid reasons to own annuities as part of your retirement income plans and in planning for Medicaid expenses. The key to any annuity is to understand not only the annuity but the insurance company that issues it and, in case of Medicaid-friendly annuities, your state's views on such instruments.

References

Milevsky, Moshe A. Life Annuities: An Optimal Product for Retirement Income. 2013 CFA Institute.

Rettick, Matthew J. Growth without Risk. 2011 Covenant Reliance Producers.

Takacs, Timothy. Please Read this before you Buy a Medicaid Friendly Annuity. Retrieved from http://www.tn-elderlaw.com/family_resources/read_this_before_you_buy_an_annuity.

Watkins, James W. Variable Annuities, Reading Between the Lines. Retrieved from http://www.investsense.com/variable-annuities.

Weisman, Steven. Truth about Buying Annuities. 2009 Pearson Education, Inc.

About Kirk G. Meyer

Kirk G. Meyer's educational and work background is relatively diverse. Currently, Kirk is working on his Doctorate in Business Administration from William Howard Taft University. Kirk has completed an M.S. in Financial Planning from Bentley University in suburban Boston, Massachusetts, and is now an investment advisor in the State of Tennessee in addition to working for the government in the area of contracts. Kirk also holds a B.S. in Business Administration from Haskell Indian Nations University in Lawrence, Kansas, and an MBA and M.S. in Accounting from Strayer University in Washington, DC. Before Kirk's current position, Kirk was a bank examiner for a federal regulatory agency. In addition to Kirk's education and work experience, he is also a registered independent life insurance agent in his home state of Tennessee, able to advise on various life insurance and annuity products to individuals and families in need of these types of services.

Kirk's educational background and love of helping others make him an asset to those looking for assistance and guidance in financial and personal financial matters. Kirk resides in Nashville, Tennessee, with his lovely wife.

One Last Chance for the Free Gifts!

Again, as a big thank you for getting A Brief Overview of Annuities, I want to offer you some valuable gifts and a chance to get some on-going financial advice. Just for getting this book, it entitles you to my Budget Spreadsheet and Debt Reduction Spreadsheet that I normally sell for a total of $10. It is yours free for getting A Brief Overview of Annuities and signing up for my free email newsletters that have previews to my ebooks. These special articles are geared towards personal finance and now access to these two useful spreadsheets. To get your spreadsheets, now go to my blog's website and sign up today. Visit http://bit.ly/KGMLetter today to get your free valuable spreadsheets.

If you enjoyed this book, I would appreciate it very much if you could leave a review on Amazon.com. Please go to http://amzn.to/1Lo7Mwh to leave your review.

How to Contact Kirk G. Meyer

Feel free to email Kirk at kirk@kgmeyerpc.com.

Please follow Kirk's blog at www.kgmeyerpc.com, and he welcomes any comments or suggestions on how to make his blog or books better for you.

You can also follow Kirk on Twitter at @kirkgmeyer

You can follow Kirk on Facebook at www.facebook.com/kgmeyerpc

You can follow Kirk on LinkedIn at www.linkedin.com/in/kirkgmeyer

You can follow Kirk on Pinterest at https://www.pinterest.com/kirkgmeyer/

You can follow Kirk on Instagram at https://www.instagram.com/kirkgmeyer/

For a complete listing of Kirk's books, please visit his Amazon Author Page at Kirk G Meyer.

Goodreads at https://www.goodreads.com/kirkgmeyer

Other Books by Kirk G. Meyer

Thrift Savings Plan: A Practical Guide to the TSP

The Basics of Life Insurance

A Brief Overview of Annuities

Financial Plans: Just the Basics

Personal Finance: A Grouping of Financial Topics

Final Expense Insurance

Budgeting 101

The Basics of Life Insurance and Annuities Bundle

Your Credit Report and You

The Basics of Personal Finance

Investing 101: A Basic Guide to Investing for Beginners

How the Stock Market Operates

401(k) Retirement Loans: Loans that can cost you more than you know

Basics of Personal Finance: How to Maintain a Financial Strategy

101 Powerful Tips for Legally Improving Your Credit Score

Preview for Basics of Life Insurance

First, let's examine the most common type of life insurance, and that is term insurance. As the name implies, the insurance is normally in place for a period of 5, 10, 15, 20, or 30 years. This insurance is usually the least expensive, as it provides a death benefit only and does not accumulate any cash value. The policy will help provide security for the named beneficiary in the event the insured dies, and the coverage is only for the length of the term. If the insured does not die during the term, no benefits will be observed, and the cost of the policy will be the premiums paid to the insurance company. A term policy is used when coverage is needed only for a certain period or if the insured has limited funds available for life insurance. As the policy does not accumulate any assets and is for a limited period, the premiums will be lower than that of a permanent insurance product. By design, the lower premiums paid will allow the insured to obtain a higher face value for the death benefit. As the insured gets older and chooses to renew the policy, the premiums will be higher, which is a negative aspect of term insurance. But if the insured is younger, term insurance can provide a large death benefit at a very reasonable premium cost.

Some term policies renew on an annual basis, with the premiums increasing every year, while others renew on the anniversary of the expiration of the term. Also, most term policies are convertible to permanent policies at the option of the insured for a fee. Both of these options are available without providing proof of insurability, since the insured already has a policy with the company, and thereby additional underwriting is not necessary. There is an advantage of purchasing a term policy when younger and, in theory, healthier, than when older and more difficult to insure due to health concerns. In that instance, a term policy not only provides security for the insured's family but enables one to convert a term policy to a permanent one when they otherwise might be unable to obtain the insurance.

The premiums paid for term insurance are considered level since they do not change as long as the policy is in effect. If the policy is a 30-year term policy, the premiums will be consistent for the entire 30 year period. An annual term is guaranteed for one year but is not a level term policy due to its year by year nature and the fact that the premiums will increase every year it renews. Any time a policy is renewed, the insurance company will adjust the premiums to a higher amount due to the increased likelihood the insured could die during the policy. That is one reason term insurance is so reasonable for younger people and young families starting; the likelihood that death will occur during the term is lower than for an older person. For term insurance, the longer the term is, the higher the premium will be, again due to the likelihood that the insured could die during the term's period. Generally, a ten-year term policy's premium would be less expensive than a 30-year term policy for the same individual.

There is also a second type of term policy, and that is one with a decreasing term. These policies generally have a level premium, but the death benefit will decrease over time. They are used as mortgage protection products for people seeking to protect their primary residence if death occurs before paying off the mortgage.

The next four insurance types will be permanent insurance products, as compared to the term product. The main differences between permanent and term insurance are that permanent insurance policies generally have higher premiums, may have constant level premiums over the life of the policy, build cash value, and cover the life of the insured. Now let's look at the four main types of permanent life insurance.

Whole life insurance provides the insured with guaranteed insurance protection for the life of the insured or until premium payments cease. Unlike term insurance, whole life has a cash value component to it that makes owning the life insurance policy an asset. A portion of the premium goes to pay for the life insurance, and a portion goes to making up the cash value, which has a guaranteed minimum rate of return that grows tax-deferred. Like term insurance, the premium is level for the life of the policy, and the death benefit is a known constant.

The premium for a whole life policy is a multi-part premium. First, part of the premium goes to pay for the life insurance itself; second, there are administrative fees that the insurance company charges; and finally, part of it goes to the investment component of the policy or the cash value. Gains in the cash value are tax-deferred and basing the taxes on your cost basis when you withdraw the funds. For example, if your cash value is $100,000 and your cost basis was $80,000, you are only liable for taxes on the $20,000 difference between the two values. The basis is calculated by premiums paid by you, minus dividends, and any previous withdrawals, if applicable. The amount of a withdrawal that is over your basis is taxed as ordinary income and not at a capital gains rate. As this policy is permanent, the premium is higher. After the insured has accumulated substantial cash value, he can use that pool of money to pay premiums until such time that the value decreases to zero. This type of policy is both an insurance policy and a savings account.

Universal life is another type of permanent life insurance that is similar to whole life in certain respects, but it is considered a flexible or adjustable life. Like whole life, it is a permanent policy that accumulates a cash value component based on current interest rates. Unlike whole life, universal life allows the insured to adjust the death benefit as personal needs change. The premiums are also adjustable depending on the level of the death benefit that the insured desires, resulting in higher premiums for a higher death benefit, and a lower premium for a lower death benefit. Also, the premiums are adjustable to match the death benefit and the value accumulated in the cash value portion. That does not mean someone who purchases a universal life product has to adjust the death benefits or premiums, but it is an alternative to whole life where both are set at the beginning of the policy.

Variable life is the third type of permanent life insurance, which is similar to whole life and made up of two components. One is the life insurance benefit, and the other is a savings feature that is allowed to grow in certain investment vehicles. On one side is the general account, which consists of the portion of the premiums that go towards paying for the life insurance death benefit and is not allocated to anyone policy that the company issues. The other component has various investment funds that are within the insurance company's investment profile, consisting of equities, money markets, bonds, or any combination. Due to the investment portion of the product, the cash value and death benefit have the possibility of fluctuating, hence the name variable life. This life insurance product is different from whole life and universal life. Classified as a security and, therefore, must be sold by a licensed life insurance agent as well as a licensed securities dealer.

The fourth and final permanent life insurance product is variable universal life. This product allows the insured to adjust the premiums and death benefits, and still have the flexibility of investing excess funds for growth. Like the variable type of permanent policies, this one is also classified as an investment and thereby must be sold not only by a licensed life insurance agent but also as a licensed securities dealer. That means variable and variable universal policies are regulated by both the state in which issued and the Securities and Exchange Commission. In these policies, all of the risks lie with the insured and not the insurance company, which means that the death benefit may go up or down depending on the success of the investments made by the insured. Many insurance companies that issue this type of policy may also issue some kind of guarantee that at least a minimum death benefit is paid to the policy's beneficiary, except for variable universal life.

Many people want permanent life insurance but need a higher death benefit for a certain period. While a universal life policy allows the insured to change the death benefit, it may not be the most practical or economical choice of products. As an alternative, the insured can buy a whole life policy for the amount they expect to need in their senior years and buy a term policy at the same time to cover the need for a higher death benefit for that period. This approach is normally cheaper and makes more sense than buying the higher-priced universal life policy by itself.

www.ingramcontent.com/pod-product-compliance
Lightning Source LLC
Chambersburg PA
CBHW070514220526
45467CB00002B/652